When I Am

Carmela Leung

BookLeaf Publishing

Presentation by *BookLeaf Publishing*

Web: www.bookleafpub.com

E-mail: info@bookleafpub.com

ISBN: 9789357615839

First edition 2022

ACKNOWLEDGEMENT

A special thank you to my lovely friend Teann for helping me out with the cover!

And thank you to all the people who've ever read my writing and told me it mattered. That's how we got here.

PREFACE

Hello there,

Welcome to a tiny sliver of my world! I hope you find what you're looking for in your stay, whether that be belonging, learning, or something else entirely.

Remember: if you've met (or in this case, read about) one autistic person, you've met one autistic person. Autism is a greenhouse that looks and feels different for each of us, and it's not up to us what plants flourish within. There will be similarities, there will be differences, and, well, doesn't that just make us human?

Take care,
Carmela

When I am autistic

The world is like an orchestra
That proudly plays its piece
Together, different parts perform
A tune that does not cease

The strings with runs and winds with trills
The horns, they seem to sing
A rising sun, a cresting dawn
In harmony they bring

A dazzling movement touches hearts
So powerful and strong
But when so bold, it's clear to see
If just one note goes wrong

Then chaos loud, cacophony
A world of overwhelm
The rhyme and rhythm fall apart
It's all so much... too much...

The world is like an orchestra
I sometimes wish it weren't
For when my fires all burn so bright
Well, then I just get burnt

When I am in a classroom

The person in front of me is bouncing their leg
The one beside shifts their arm, shifts their arm,
shifts their arm
There are blinking lights somewhere just out of
sight
The person in front of me is bouncing their leg
The light is blinking somewhere to my left
The door opens and closes itself in an unseen
wind
The person in front of me is bouncing their leg
The person in front of me is bouncing their leg
Shifts their arm
Blinking lights
Bouncing their leg
bouncing their leg
blink blink
leg
arm
open
leg
close
leg
blink
arm
leg

the door in front of me is blinking their arm
the light beside shifts their door
The person in front of me is bouncing their leg

When I am emptying the dishwasher

Ceramic xylophones and tinny silverware
chimes greet me as I pull open the dishwasher
Tawny cupboards observe from above, dark
wood grain a mirror for the maze of alabaster
below
I close my eyes, glimpsing orderly stacks
through closed doors to sketch a map in my
mind
Rice grain pattern bowls adorned with blue
dragons nestled in the top left
Rimmed dinner plates with faded gold edges
towering in the bottom right
Red and orange chopsticks tossed haphazardly
into baskets in the drawer

And at last the work of emptying the racks
begins:
Select each dish by size
Envision its home
Chart a path
Every movement deliberate
Every arrangement perfect

When I am trying to sit still

5

Snowflake panic drifts down
Churned up by the spinning in my chest
Eagerly filling my toes, my ankles, my knees
I twist to wring the anxiety from my legs

I want to sink into the ground
Let my bones run like mountaintop rills
I am a songbird piloting a mechanoid
These rusted hinges are not in tune

When I am introduced to a pet in a video call

In your presence, the rest of the world turns to
pixelated sludge
And the spotlight my brain declares is always on
me changes focus
Delight takes root and happy flaps make it grow
Hello! hello! hello! the seed pods burst in chorus
Can you see these electric blossoms bloom?

When I am infodumping

Do you know how caffeine works in your brain?
Can you please ask me so I can explain?
How about fairy rings? May I please share
Why grass on this circle is greener than there?

Bring up a topic that interests me so
And watch as I tell you the things that I know!
Pouring out all of these facts I collect!
Taking great interest in how they connect!!

Adenosine's stuff that your body will make,
One of its jobs: to make you take a break,
And so caffeine, chemically, is *similar* to
adenosine, which means it
can bind to those receptors(!), so that *stops* the
adenosine from
being able to do that, and not only that, but–

Sorry
I sometimes gct carried away
The world's full of beauty, I learn every day
To show my affection, I share what I learn
And eagerly await what you'll share in return

When I am misunderstood during a conversation

Clay sculpture crumbling
Jumble of me puzzle pieces scattered
Strewn across the grate floor of this glass box
Tumbling away as I swipe fruitlessly at them

Shapes so carefully selected cracked
Corners blunted, round edges flattened
Once-connected fragments now strangers
No glue is strong enough to bind lost pieces

Bottomless rift growing with every fragment
consumed
There was never a bridge here
Only a glass box hanging on for dear life
What am I meant to do when my best is not
enough?

When I am expecting an email

I carefully weave my schedule
Every colour has its place
Every to-do accounted for

I check my email once
The strings twist a little
As I redo part of the tapestry

I check my email twice
The strings catch at the ends
As I readjust my image

I check my email five times
The strings coil together
As I fumble with the knots

I check my email ten times
The strings begin to fray
As I claw at the rat's nest

I check my email again
I check my email again
I check my email again

I check my email again
The strings hold my knuckles hostage
As I flail like an out-of-control puppet
Empty loom standing over a failed game of cat's
cradle

When I am listening to the rain

I breathe in the music of clouds come to greet me

.

.

.

Taste the percussive tapdance against my bedroom window

.

.

.

Raindrops make abstract the view outside

.

.

.

And fill my veins with a cashmere tingle

.

.

.

When I am given directions to a meeting spot

My body's here, my mind is there
My eyes are closed but still I stare
At where your words are pointing me
The world you paint is what I see

I soar along the campus street
As you describe the place we'll meet
Fly through the arches growing green
With benches where your friends convene

That hall is what I'm looking for
Then to the right, there is a door
It's right beside where people eat
Or get a drink and take a seat

No need for North or South - I know
Exactly where I need to go
Excited, for the time draws near
When I shall get to meet you here!

When I am having dinner on campus

Snowglobe of chatter envelopes me
Thunderstorm erupting from below
It is all one sweeping maelstrom
Yet each voice contributes to the whelm-o-meter
And everything wants to join

Silverware clinks chairs scrape lights buzz doors
slam laughter rings blenders drone bags rustle
feet shuffle plastic snaps drinks slosh hands
smack shoes tap cans pop griddles sizzle coins
jingle mouths chew ventilation hums
microwaves beep

My friend tries to speak to me
Her words but a thread in a bristling, itchy
carpet
Woven from the cacophony of this building
Fibers stretch from every brick and tile
A spider's web constricting

When I am in a remote meeting

The meeting has the 9 of us, a grid of 3 times 3
This pattern-seeking brain I have, it scans
subconsciously
It's not what I should focus on, yet here is what I
see:

The people with the longest hair all wore it up
today
The folks who have their glasses form a 2-by-2
array
And somehow everybody's top is largely shades
of grey

The universe makes art in little ways that others
miss
To them it doesn't matter but for me, it brings me
bliss
So if I bring it up, I hope my joy, you won't
dismiss

When I am in a crowd

There are so many people here
And I am lost now
I know where I am
But I am lost
I have made a maze of nothing
Answers warped and smouldering
Marbles spinning on the floor
Jacks tumbling in every direction
I don't know what I lost but
I am lost

When I am playing piano

The music is my friend
It holds my hands and talks me through how I
feel
Probing into fog an emotions wheel cannot clear
We adventure to another world
And as we chat, there is nothing that goes over
my head

But still, conversations must draw to a close
So we fly back to this wrong planet
Fold the grey blanket back over
Return the keys that allowed this escape
I will visit again, dear friend

When I am trying to say the right thing

Plinko board sat upon an iron spring
Jack-in-the-box knocking helium balloons about
It is a treacherous journey between my thoughts
and words

It slips between my fingers and flies over my
head
The tip of my tongue is pinned down by
everything on it
How am I meant to grab hold of nothing and
craft something?

When enough meaning has bled out
I settle for the husks that remain
They are light enough to hand over to somebody
else
It is a treacherous journey between my thoughts
and words

When I am changing water bottles (or not)

So there's this water bottle that I've had for
many years
It's by my side most everyday, seen laughs and
even tears
The bright green paint a constant as I move
through many lives
Each dent and nick a story of the fumbles it
survives

The paint is getting chipped, though, and the
bottom's coming loose
The sealing on the cap is getting worse with
every use
It spills whenever it gets tipped; from where, it's
never clear
I don't know how to fix it - is its deadline
drawing near?

I got this brand new bottle, and I guess I'd say
it's fine
It mocks my dear green bottle with its modern,
sleek design
But still, it is a stranger, it's a change that I can't
stand

I'm sorry, newer bottle, but the old one stays in
hand

'Cause what if it gets lonely while it's sitting on
its own?
Or will it get upset at me for leaving it alone?
I know it's not alive but still, it might get sad or
scared
And think that I've forgotten all the memories
we shared

When I am meeting someone new

Who do these people expect me to be?
What parts of me do I want them to see?
What if they don't like the words that I use?
What if my care seems like naught but a ruse?
Will they perceive me as childish or rude?
Will I seem difficult, stuck "in a mood"?
Does my anxiety make me aloof?
What about stims, do those make me a goof?

"Just be yourself! Do your best to be you!"
What does that mean? I don't know what to do
I'm trying to mimic, sponge up what seems
"right"
Even if that makes me look too uptight
'Cause here's what I've learned: sometimes
different's too scary
It makes those around me become sort of weary
An alien trying to blend in - that's me
And every try takes my spoons as a fee

When I am sitting too close to strangers

The crickets' dialogue I do not resent
I eavesdrop on the gossiping ducks
Hold my seed-filled palms out for the birds
Pay little mind to the thorns that scratch my
arms

But when two strangers squeeze onto the bench
beside me
I cannot help but feel upset by their chatter
ringing through my skull
Anxiety builds as they creep closer and closer
Their every movement echoing in our shared
seat

Don't touch me
Don't touch me
Don't touch me
Would it be rude of me to leave?

When I am learning about you

"Small talk" is defined as:
"A polite conversation about unimportant
matters"
What's important changes
I think sometimes we forget this

I want to hear about your weekend
It tells me what you enjoy doing
Keep telling me about that meal
So I might know what you find tasty
Share about your favourite show
Teach me what draws you in
Give your opinion on the weather
When I see your favourite, I'll think of you

I don't like small talk, that is true
But you make this conversation important

When I am in a lecture

The professor claps her hand over the
microphone
    feedback feedbACK FEEDBACK FEEdback
And continues the lecture
She is talking about how to solve a problem
    louder louder loudER LOUDER LOUder
But the only thing I can focus on
Is when the next
    scree scree scREE SCREE SCREE SCRee
Will come

Unexpectedly
My heart is pounding and I am
    screaming scrEAMING SCREAMING
Silently

When I am human

They look at me, surprised
Not quite green or antennaed or misplaced
enough to be alien
"Aren't we all a little autistic?"

Aren't all birds a bit penguin?
Aren't all trees kind of aspens?
Aren't all mammals sort of platypuses?

Or maybe:
Aren't we all human?

Printed in the USA
CPSIA information can be obtained
at www.ICGtesting.com
LVHW011247130324
774240LV00014B/888